ESSENCE OF ETERNITY

A 40-Day Devotional

Mavis Sutton

AuthorHouse™ UK Ltd.
500 Avebury Boulevard
Central Milton Keynes, MK9 2BE
www.authorhouse.co.uk
Phone: 08001974150

Published by AuthorHouse 5/11/2012

ISBN: 978-1-4678-9646-7 (sc)
ISBN: 978-1-4678-9645-0 (e)

Foreword

Mavis Sutton was born in 1932 in a little village nestled between the rugged hills of Derbyshire's Peak District. Growing up in a poor but happy and hardworking home, she gained first a scholarship to grammar school and then to drama school. After leaving drama school Mavis accepted Christ as her Saviour and Lord, and immediately felt God's call on her life to Christian ministry. Abandoning the acting career that beckoned, she began training and ministering in her native Peak District in the heart of England, as a Methodist lay-preacher. She went on to do further studies at Edinburgh's Faith Mission Bible College, being greatly encouraged by the ministry of the College Principal, Duncan Campbell, whom God had used in the Hebrides Revival.

After College, Mavis served for two years with Faith Mission, evangelizing in Ireland. Hearing God's call to the indigenous tribes of Brazil's Amazon rain forest, she joined the Unevangelized Fields Mission, and worked for some years as a single woman deep in the jungle amongst Kayapo Indians. She married and later returned to the UK with her husband Alfred, a Pastor and fellow missionary, and her son, and served two congregations in the Westcountry. After Alfred's death in 1996 she spent some time with Operation Mobilisation, serving on the mission ship, the MV Doulos, as it visited ports in South-East Asia and the Arabian Gulf.

She now lives in North Devon, in a cottage a stone's throw from the Atlantic Ocean. Mavis continues to preach, run a global-prayer group, and to dream of serving Christ in far-flung places.

I passionately commend this book to you, not least because Mavis Sutton is a person who has deeply impacted my life. It is largely through her love and example that I have come to love Jesus and enjoy a life grounded in God. And so I must confess that I am a little biased, as Mavis is my Mother!

The following are reflections, stories and snippets gleaned from a lifetime's ministry and experiences at home and abroad, from a lady who has walked with Jesus. They are offered with the prayer that you may be encouraged in your relationship with the One who loves you and calls you to share His love with others, or as my Mum puts it, "to permeate the courts of time with essence of eternity."

Rev. Tim Sutton, London – Easter 2012

A Prayer

Breathe your love into my soul
O Lord of earth and sky.
I need your love to win the lost
And talk of Calvary.

Breathe your peace into my mind
When troubles wear my life.
I need your peace, a heart at rest
From sin and self and strife.

Breathe your joy into my heart
In tests and trials sore;
The joy that knows no boundaries
And longs for heaven more.

Breathe your faith upon my lips
When in your name I pray,
The faith that claims your promises
And walks the Spirit way.

Breathe your power into my frame
O God of Pentecost!
All other power unsanctified
Is but to me as dross.

Moment by moment give your grace
That I may fragrant be,
To permeate the courts of time
With essence of eternity.

-Mavis Sutton

DAY 1 – Rising Up

"Even youths grow tired and weary, and young men stumble and fall; but those who hope in the LORD will renew their strength. They will soar on wings like eagles; they will run and not grow weary, they will walk and not be faint."

ISAIAH 40:30-31

The eagle is mentioned 32 times in Scripture. The characteristics of this amazing bird are emphasised by God again and again. A great eagle was once observed flying across a lake in less than one minute. It was a lake 2 miles wide, and the average speed of the flight was 150 miles per hour. The eagle soars up to a height of half a mile, and scans an area of about 4.5 square miles. After spotting his prey, he turns sharply, folds his wings into a tight, aero-dynamic formation, and begins to dive at a speed of up to 200 miles per hour. An eagle may have up to 7,182 feathers! Each year, he is totally renewed, replacing every single feather in his entire body, over a period of several months. The eagle's feathers are renewed and replaced in such a way that the bird is not stopped from soaring. His primary feathers are separated at the tips, like fingers of a hand, and air passes more quickly over the tops of the wings than the bottom, enabling him to fly almost indefinitely. Turbulent winds enable the eagle to fly high and higher, allowing the bird a larger view of the earth beneath. The higher he flies, the fewer the distractions.

Do you get the picture?

Lord Jesus, help me to wait upon you, so that I may run and not be weary, walk and not faint: to soar up on the wings of prayer, through the winds of turbulence and change, leaving all distractions behind.

DAY 2 - Are You Troubled?

'He said to them, "Why are you troubled, and why do doubts rise in your minds?""

LUKE 24:38

Does the past trouble us? Do we spend a lot of time worrying about it? Do we worry about our unfulfilled vows, opportunities that slipped away, unpardoned sins? The good news is that the past can be dealt with by the blood of Jesus. "If we confess our sins, he is faithful and just and will forgive us our sins and purify us from all unrighteousness" (I John 1:9).

Does the present trouble us? Family upsets, unemployment, financial problems, unstable world governments, disasters, tragedies on every hand? Dark days are part of our earthly experience. When we became Christians, God never promised "roses, roses all the way." What He did promise was His Presence every moment of every day, through thick and thin.

Does the future trouble us? Pain, grief, loneliness, old age, poverty, persecution? "Cast all your anxiety on him because he cares for you" (I Peter 5:7).

How many "Fear Not's" are there in the Scripture? Some say there are 365 plus one extra for a leap-year! Whatever the number is, the fact remains that the Bible is full of commands and reasons why the believer should not be afraid.

"And even to your old age I am he; and even to hoar hairs will I carry you: I have made, and I will bear; even I will carry, and will deliver you" (Isaiah 46:4, KJV).

Why on earth should we be troubled about anything, when Jesus has promised that nothing is able to separate us from His love (Romans 8:38-39)?

DAY 3 – Are You Ready?

"They were looking intently up into the sky as he was going, when suddenly two men dressed in white stood beside them. "Men of Galilee," they said, "why do you stand here looking into the sky? This same Jesus, who has been taken from you into heaven, will come back in the same way you have seen him go into heaven."

Acts 1:10-11

There was never any doubt in my mind that God was the Creator. The proof of there being a Creator lay all around me, in the lovely Peak District National Park which was my home. The rolling hills, deep dales, verdant woods, hidden valley, gaping caverns and great limestone cliffs – as well as the vast mushroom fields, cob nut bushes – not to speak of the lapwings and blackbirds – everything in the world of nature proclaimed a Creator. I used to walk for miles, praying aloud, praising God for His wonderful world. But – I didn't know Jesus as my Saviour. Then, when I was 21, one evening, in the old Methodist Chapel, He made himself known to me, saved me and called me into His service.

I remember so well that I needed to buy some boots before winter came. But, having learned that Jesus was to come back to earth, and maybe soon, I refused to buy them.

I thought to myself, 'There'd be no time to wear them. What a waste of money!' That's how much I believed that He was about to come back to earth.

The years have rolled by, and still, He hasn't come. But, my Bible tells me that this same Jesus, the one who saved me, will come back again, although neither I, nor anyone else, know the date. He will come again to earth, not like that first time when He came to Bethlehem, but with all His holy angels! The skies will roll back, and Jesus will come, in all His glory, to judge the earth! The archangel, Gabriel, will shout and awaken the dead in Christ; the sea and the earth will give up bodies that will be raised and glorified! The trumpet of God will sound (that is the 'last trump,' signalling, 'move out')! The dead in Christ will rise and every living believer will be caught up and raptured, that is, changed in the twinkling of an eye, to meet Christ in the air! All this is recorded in I Thessalonians 4:16-17.

Are you ready for this momentous occasion, His coming again?

DAY 4 – Seeing His Glory

"The Word became flesh and made his dwelling among us. We have seen his glory, the glory of the One and Only, who came from the Father, full of grace and truth."

JOHN 1:14

Man needed a Saviour, so God stepped out of eternity into time. No wonder there was a special light set in the heavens when He was born!

No wonder that Heaven's angels conversed with humble Shepherds!

No wonder there were special revelations, through dreams!

No wonder – because God was sending His one and only Son, on that night of miracles, to be the Saviour of the World!

God became Man –

Born of a woman, He grew up as an adolescent; worked as a carpenter; was hungry, angry, sleepy, weary, thirsty, poor, experienced pain, tempted (but never gave into temptation), shared earth's sorrows – all that we may enjoy the treasures of Heaven for all eternity.

He trod earth's dusty paths that we may tread the golden streets of glory.

Some years ago a missionary engaged in translation, accompanied the Indians on a journey into the forest. They came to a ravine and it seemed as though they would have to give up; but out came the machetes and, soon, they had cut down a tree which they made into a bridge across the chasm. The translator realised that the word the Indians used for "bridge" was the word he needed for "reconciliation." Jesus is the "bridge" from earth to Heaven.

Meditate on the measures God has taken to make Himself known to you.

DAY 5 - What Is Your Life?

"Now listen, you who say, "Today or tomorrow we will go to this or that city, spend a year there, carry on business and make money." Why, you do not even know what will happen tomorrow. What is your life? You are a mist that appears for a little while and then vanishes. Instead, you ought to say, "If it is the Lord's will, we will live and do this or that."

JAMES 4:13-15

James says life is like a mist – here for a little while, and then – gone!

Every morning, in the Amazon rain forest, I would wake up to a thick mist. The tall trees around the Indian encampment would seem almost "out of this world" and spectre-like. I would hear voices, dogs barking, cocks crowing, birds singing, water splashing, babies crying, monkeys howling, crickets chattering, toads gulping – and see nothing – because everything was enveloped in a mysterious morning mist.

But wait awhile! A few short hours and then... that jungle mist had vanished and all seemed normal once again.

James compares our mortality with withering grass (James 1:10), and says our lives are just like a mist that is seen for a little while and then vanishes (James 4:14)! Very brief, in comparison with trees and hills that we know have endured for centuries.

"Life at best is very brief,

Like the falling of a leaf"

In light of this, how will you live today?

DAY 6 - My Life Is Borrowed

"For this very reason, Christ died and returned to life so that he might be the Lord of both the dead and the living. You, then, why do you judge your brother? Or why do you look down on your brother? For we will all stand before God's judgment seat. It is written:"'As surely as I live,' says the Lord, 'every knee will bow before me; every tongue will confess to God."' So then, each of us will give an account of himself to God."

ROMANS 14:9-12

Other Scriptures confirm that our life is not our own:

Job 12:10 says, "In his hand is the life of every creature and the breath of all mankind."

Ezekiel 18:4 says, "For every living soul belongs to me."

Ecclesiastes 12:7 says, "the dust returns to the ground it came from, and the spirit returns to God who gave it."

I am a steward of my life. Anything borrowed must be returned. George Matheson had this in mind when he wrote "I give Thee back the life I owe." One day we shall have to give an account of the way in which we have lived our short lives.

I am dependent upon God for my next breath, my heart (pumping 1.6 million gallons of blood across 12,000 miles of arterial highways - the distance between New York and Hong Kong, via the Panama Canal) will go on pulsating until God allows it to stop. My brain, which retains, receives, deduces and responds, will continue to function until my Maker says, "No more." My hand, which no tool or die-maker could duplicate perfectly, will continue to direct, hold, form and comfort until the day that God says, "That's enough." My ears, which He gave me – 24,000 cords, capable of distinguishing 500 different sounds in a second – will hear, while God allows.

All I am is a steward of my life.

DAY 7 - My Life Is Bought

"Do you not know that your body is a temple of the Holy Spirit, who is in you, whom you have received from God? You are not your own; you were bought at a price. Therefore honour God with your body."

I CORINTHIANS 6:19-20

I am indebted to God because His Son, Jesus, bought me with His precious blood, when He died for me on Calvary – that's redemption!

It was about midday. The sun was at its zenith. There was a clap of hands at the front door. My eleven-year old son went to the door of our little Brazilian home. Two lads stood there, carrying a home-made wooden cage in which was a struggling, tiny, beautiful blue bird.

"Quer comprar?" (Will you buy?)

"Quanto?" (How much?)

"Vinte cruzeiros!" (20 pence)

"Sim, compro." (Yes, I'll buy it)

My son fetched the money from his room, and paid. He carried the cage to the back door, opened the cage, and freed the tiny captive.

I watched as that little songster soared up into a bright blue sky, singing as it soared, flying back to the forest where it belonged. And I thought – That's redemption! The price was paid to set me free!

Hallelujah!

DAY 8 - God Has A Plan For You

"For I know the plans I have for you," declares the LORD,
"plans to prosper you and not to harm you,
plans to give you hope and a future."

JEREMIAH 29:11

We make plans. When they go wrong, we get disappointed. We all have hopes and dreams and expectations – when they come to nothing, we sometimes despair.

But God has a plan for you and a plan for me – a much better plan than we could draw up for ourselves! It is a very special plan, and, when we ask Him to be our Saviour and Friend, His plan begins to be realised.

A six year-old, called Amy, used to pray, every night, that God would give her blue eyes instead of the brown ones He had given her. She loved the Lord Jesus. Her parents had taught her that God answers prayer. So each morning, she would look intently into her mirror, to see if God had answered the prayer of her heart. And – He never did! Years later, when Amy was a young missionary in India she knew why! She could secretly thread her way into the heathen temple to rescue boys and girls from abuse – why? Because of her brown eyes! With her coffee-stained skin and native dress and the BROWN eyes, she could be unrecognised, and come away from the temple with children who needed her love and protection, and to whom she told the stories of Jesus.

Don't miss the plan that God has for YOU!

We all make plans and sometimes they are not for our good, because we don't have the blue-print for our lives, as God has. His plans for us are very special, and far better, than those we draw up for ourselves! Why don't you bow before Him, just now, and thank Him for His perfect plans?

DAY 9 - Don't Be Afraid!

"Ignoring what they said, Jesus told the synagogue ruler, "Don't be afraid; just believe."

MARK 5:36

What are you afraid of? I'm afraid of the doctor, the dentist, the surgeon and pain!

I used to be afraid of school exams, change, moving house, amongst other things. I was afraid of killing a snake; afraid to canoe down river, over rapids, with the Brazilian Indians because they didn't believe I couldn't swim; afraid of the rats as they ran along the rafters of my little mud house by the Xingu river; afraid, sometimes, of the wild tribe amongst whom I had made my home.

I had to keep in mind that Jesus said, "Don't be afraid; just believe." Those were the words as he spoke to Jairus about his dying 12 year old daughter.

Jairus had come to plead that Jesus might visit his home and bring healing. Then there was an interruption, as Jesus began to accompany him to his home. A few minutes later Jairus was told that his little daughter was dead so there was no point in "bothering" Jesus any longer – it was all over! But the Saviour turned to Jairus and said, "Don't be afraid; just believe!" We have to read between the lines, and imagine Jairus' reaction as Jesus went into the child's room and took her hand, saying, "Little girl, get up." She did get up and she did walk around, and I'm sure that Jairus believed!

Do *you*?

DAY 10 - My Shepherd

"The LORD is my shepherd, I shall not be in want. He makes me lie down in green pastures, he leads me beside quiet waters, he restores my soul. He guides me in paths of righteousness for his name's sake. Even though I walk through the valley of the shadow of death I will fear no evil, for you are with me; your rod and your staff, they comfort me."

PSALM 23:1-4

Such a well-loved psalm! Read on various public occasions – marriages, deaths, anniversaries and so on. Charles Spurgeon called it "The Pearl of Psalms." "The Lord is my shepherd," says David – Mine! It was a personal affirmation of his faith. We can hear him thinking, as he watched the sheep, "Just as these sheep are in my care, so I am in my Shepherd's care." Sheep – weak, foolish defenceless and dependent. The Shepherd – strong, wise, protective and the provider of pasture.

If He is not yet yours, you can make Him yours today; this moment, even!

You rightly belong to the Good Shepherd, who gave His life for the Sheep.

Do you *really* belong to Him? Can you say, "He's mine!"

Have you come to Him, the old-fashioned way – the way of the Cross? There is only one way! Jesus said, "I am the way" (John 14:6). His Name is the only, "name under heaven given to men by which we must be saved" (Acts 4:12). There is, "no other mediator between God and men; but the man Christ Jesus" (I Timothy 2:5).

"Mine, mine, mine

I know thou art mine!

Saviour, dear Saviour

I know thou art mine!"

The great and mighty God has taken upon Himself the characteristics of a Shepherd.

DAY 11 - Help Me

"All your commands are trustworthy; help me, for men persecute me without cause."

PSALM 119:86

If only we would make this our daily prayer! "Help me!"

We pretend to be self-sufficient, independent. How much richer our lives would be if we confessed our utter dependence upon the Lord Jesus!

Lord Jesus, help me today:

Help me to solve this problem – I'm trying to find the answer myself;

To ride this storm that is raging and causing the little craft of my life to founder;

Help me to heal that broken relationship.

To keep Satan at bay;

To rise above my circumstances;

To love that unlovely one;

To respond to my neighbours' need;

To intercede for the lost;

To be patient in trials;

To be sensitive to your Spirit's leading;

To depend entirely upon you;

To keep my eyes on you, Jesus!

"For I am the LORD, your God, who takes hold of your right hand and says to you, Do not fear; I will help you" (Isaiah 41:13).

DAY 12 - A Lesson From The Coney

"Four things on earth are small, yet they are extremely wise: Ants are creatures of little strength, yet they store up their food in the summer; coneys are creatures of little power, yet they make their home in the crags..."

PROVERBS 30:24-26

The coney (also known as the Hyrax or Rock Badger) lives only in Bible Lands, so many of us have never seen one. It's about the size of a rabbit and has a brownish yellow fur coat with a spot of yellow on its back. The Bible tells us three things about them:

One, they are very weak, because they don't have anything with which to protect themselves – no nails, no claws, no horns, no tusks, no teeth, so they are quite unable to dig a hole in which to hide from danger.

Two, they make houses in the rocks; rocks that are simply there! And hideaways, behind great boulders – and there they remain safe from any danger.

Three, they are extremely wise, because they know they are weak! They don't try to make a safe place for themselves, because they realise they can't! They simply hide in the shelter that God provided for them.

I also am very weak – I can't do anything to save myself, or anything to get to Heaven. I must simply run to the Rock that God provided, the Lord Jesus. I must simply hide in Him. I can remain "in Him" and be perfectly safe and sheltered from Satan's power.

Are you "exceedingly" wise as the Coney?

DAY 13 - Pardoning Grace

"In him we have redemption through his
blood, the forgiveness of sins,
in accordance with the riches of God's
grace that he lavished on us
with all wisdom and understanding."

EPHESIANS 1:7-8

The precious blood of Christ not only ransomed and redeemed me, but it brought me forgiveness of sins!

My sins are great but His Grace is greater. Romans 5:20

God has promised to:

Cast all our sins into the depths of the sea. Micah 7:19

Remove our transgressions from us as far as the East is from the West. Psalms 103:12

Cast all our sins behind His back. Isaiah 38:17

Blot out our transgressions like a thick cloud. Isaiah 44:22

Remember our sins no more. Jeremiah 31:34

All by grace!

This is the gospel of grace that the apostle Paul preached about in Acts 20:24 as he said goodbye to the church in Ephesus. His task was to testify to "the gospel of God's grace" wherever he went. The "God of all grace" (1 Peter 5:10) has issued an invitation to the sinner, for abundant pardon that surpasses all human reasoning (Isaiah 55:6-7).

"Amazing Grace! How sweet the sound

That saved a wretch like me!

I once was lost but now am found,

Was blind, but now I see."

Live in that grace.

DAY 14 - Ready To Go

"Now we know that if the earthly tent we live in is destroyed, we have a building from God, an eternal house in heaven, not built by human hands. Meanwhile we groan, longing to be clothed with our heavenly dwelling, because when we are clothed, we will not be found naked. For while we are in this tent, we groan and are burdened, because we do not wish to be unclothed but to be clothed with our heavenly dwelling, so that what is mortal may be swallowed up by life. Now it is God who has made us for this very purpose and has given us the Spirit as a deposit, guaranteeing what is to come."

2 Corinthians 5:1-5

The following words were written by an old man, to his pastor.

"Next Sunday, you'll be talking about Heaven. I'm interested, because I have held a clear title to a property there, for many years. I didn't buy it. It was given to me, but the donor purchased it at great sacrifice.

For a long time, the great Architect of the universe has been building a home there for me, and it will never need any repairs. Termites can't eat away at its foundations, because it's built on rock. Fire can't destroy it. Floods can't wash it away. It stands, beautifully complete, ready for me to take possession and live there in peace for ever.

Between my present home and the one to which I'm going, there is a valley of deep shadows. But I'm not afraid – my Friend went through that same valley, a long time ago, and drove away all the darkness.

He has stood with me through thick and thin, and I have His promise, in printed form, that He will never leave me alone. He'll be with me, as I walk through the valley of the shadow of death. I may have already arrived at my new home by next Sunday! I don't know because my ticket to Heaven has no date on it; no return coupon, and no permit for baggage! And I'm ready to go!"

Through faith in Christ alone you too, may be "ready to go."

DAY 15 – How Great Is Our God!

"In the beginning God created the heavens and the earth."

GENESIS 1:1

Astronauts once described our planet, seen from space – 'a blue orb, unbelievably lovely.'

When we look up at the skies, lit at night, by God's silent witness the moon, we remember that He balances the planets, and that Jesus, "upholds all things by the word of his power" (Colossians 1:17). "The heavens declare the glory of God; the skies proclaim the work of his hands" (Psalm 19:1).

We learn from our text-books of the vibrations that govern musical harmonies; of the matter of the universe, existing in four different forms – solid, gas, liquid and plasma; of the way light behaves and the formation of shadows; of the miracle of growth, unseen in the dark soil; of the treasures of the snow, wind, rain, dew and sunshine; of the wealth hidden in rocks and hills – the formation, through centuries, of coal, gas and oil, beneath the seas; of the rivers, oceans, waterfalls, glaciers and fjords that can be harnessed for electricity; of the natural instincts of creatures great and small (a tiny bird, losing one third of its weight, can span the Atlantic, returning later to its original nest in some remote corner of an English hedgerow); we muse on the glowing colours of sunset and sunrise, rainbows, fish, coral reefs, moths and butterflies; and what of the perfume of a rose or a lily?

"My God, how great Thou art!"

What does it mean to you today that *this* God is *your* God?

That He has made you, too, with precision and care?

That He upholds *you*?

DAY 16 – Always Thankful

"Speak to one another with psalms, hymns and spiritual songs. Sing and make music in your heart to the Lord, always giving thanks to God the Father for everything, in the name of our Lord Jesus Christ."

EPHESIANS 5:19-20

Some time ago on a London street, I was robbed. My new handbag disappeared in a matter of seconds – with four weeks' pension to pay some bills, my watch, coach-ticket, house and car-keys, etc. An awful experience it was, too! My son, afterwards, consoled me with the words, "Never mind, Mum, I'm so thankful that whoever robbed you of your handbag, didn't rob me of you."

Well over two centuries ago, Matthew Henry, a well-known Christian teacher and commentator was also robbed. That evening, he wrote –

"Let me be thankful – first, because I was never robbed before.

Second, because whoever robbed my wallet, didn't rob me of my life

Third, although they took everything, it wasn't very much!

And fourth, because it was I who was robbed, not I who did the robbing!"

There's always something for which to be thankful!

Today, in everything, give thanks!

DAY 17 – Being Useful

"Therefore, I urge you, brothers, in view of God's mercy, to offer your bodies as living sacrifices, holy and pleasing to God—this is your spiritual act of worship."

ROMANS 12:1

Brazil is full of beautiful palm-trees! It is often called "The Land of Palms." They rise up with graceful fronds into the exotically, near unreal blue sky. There are many different varieties. I'm thinking, just now, of one called the "Carnauba," which is, say Brazilians, "The tree of life," because everything except the smell is useful!

Its oil, nuts and palmetto buds are all used as food. Its leaves are used on roofs. Its trunk is made into rafters for building houses. Its fibres are made into hammocks, threads and ropes.

And a question occurs to me: Is every part of me useful to God – my ears, mind, lips, hands, feet? If not, why not?

"All to Jesus I surrender,

All to Him I freely give

I will ever love and trust Him

In His Presence daily live

I surrender all

All to Thee, my blessed Saviour

I surrender all"

DAY 18 - From God's Recipe Book For Holy People

"But the fruit of the Spirit is love, joy, peace, patience, kindness, goodness, faithfulness, gentleness and self-control. Against such things there is no law."

GALATIANS 5:22-23

Ingredients

Oceans of love

Bucketfuls of joy

Untold quantities of peace

Endless measures of patience

Tons of kindness

Loads of goodness

Handfuls of faithfulness

Touches of gentleness

Heaps of self-control

Mix together all the ingredients with bags of concentrated prayer and generous amounts of Holy Spirit anointing-oil.

It is imperative the vessel be clean, so cleanse with tears.

Make absolutely sure the power is on and that there is a warm glow within.

Use your God-given instinct and sprinkle with lashings of praise.

The sweet aroma will permeate every room in the building and the regions beyond.

NB. This well-worn and trusted recipe will feed many hungry people and do them good!

DAY 19 - Get Rid Of The Rubbish!

"Meanwhile, the people in Judah said, "The strength of the labourers is giving out, and there is so much rubble that we cannot rebuild the wall."

NEHEMIAH 4:10

What exactly is the rubble or rubbish in our lives? Rubbish that prevents our spiritual growth – rubbish that must be cleaned out by God's word and the power of His Spirit.

Before we can rebuild we need to confess our sins and repent of them, even with tears.

What about the rubbish of prayerlessness? Spurgeon said, "As it is the business of the tailor to make clothes, and a cobbler to mend shoes, so it is the work of a Christian to pray."

What about unbelief? Rebellion against God? "For rebellion is as the sin of witchcraft, and stubbornness is as iniquity and idolatry. Because thou hast rejected the word of the LORD, he hath also rejected thee from being king" (I Sam 15:23, KJV).

And what of carnality? "The sinful mind is hostile to God. It does not submit to God's law, nor can it do so. Those controlled by the sinful nature cannot please God" (Romans 8:7).

And the rubbish of pride - what about that? "A man's pride brings him low, but a man of lowly spirit gains honour" (Proverbs 29:23). "You say, 'I am rich, I have acquired wealth and do not need a thing.' But you do not realise that you are wretched, pitiful, poor, blind and naked" (Revelation 3:17).

Pride will always say, "I can do without God." What a lie from the Evil One!

O Lord, reveal the rubbish and take it away!

DAY 20 - Waste

"Then Jesus said to his disciples, "If anyone would come after me, he must deny himself and take up his cross and follow me. For whoever wants to save his life will lose it, but whoever loses his life for me will find it. What good will it be for a man if he gains the whole world, yet forfeits his soul? Or what can a man give in exchange for his soul?"

MATTHEW 16:24-26

The tiny Piper plane lay stripped. Nearby the spear-lanced bodies of five young American missionaries half floated in the river.

It was 1956 and one of those young men was Jim Elliot, a very gifted Christian who gave up lots of legitimate activities at College, in order to keep himself wholly available for God. He had told his mother he wanted to present, "a more useful body as a living sacrifice."

Jim found himself amongst a group of young men who loved the Saviour as much as he did. With their wives, they became convinced that they must take the gospel to the Auca Indians in Ecuador, a stone-age people, who often killed for no apparent reason. A patient programme was devised, seeking to establish contact by plane, dropping gifts, showing friendliness, until the time seemed right for a face-to-face encounter with the Aucas.

It was a successful and exciting first meeting. Then came radio silence; and the discovery of the murdered bodies. What apparent waste of young lives! But Jim had written in his diary:

"He is no fool who gives what he cannot keep to gain what he cannot lose."

Lord, the world has it the wrong way around. Teach me what is true loss and true gain.

DAY 21 - Potential

"I am the gate; whoever enters through me will be saved.
He will come in and go out, and find pasture. The thief
comes only to steal and kill and destroy; I have come
that they may have life, and have it to the full."

JOHN 10:9-10

Built in 1914, the Doulos was for a long time the oldest active ocean-going passenger-ship in the world, and was affectionately known as 'The Grand Old Lady of the Seas.' The ship saw almost 95 years of service across the oceans of the world.

She was built as a cargo ship, transporting onions from New York to Texas, and yet, God had great plans for her, and rescued her from the scrap-yard.

She was then engaged in her own "rescue" mission, as a missionary ship for many years. She was true to her name – the new name that was given to her when bought by a Christian organisation:

"Doulos" – the servant!

In many ways, we Christians are like the Doulos. We were rescued by God; our lives totally changed; and, one day, we shall have a new name! (Revelation 2:17)

Our full potential is unrealised, until we accept God's offer of peace, freedom and fulfilment – all this is ours, when we enter into a personal relationship with God, through His Son, the Lord Jesus Christ, who said:

"I have come that they may have life, and have it to the full." (v10)

DAY 22 – Running Into His Arms

"He who dwells in the shelter of the Most High will rest in the shadow of the Almighty. I will say of the LORD, "He is my refuge and my fortress, my God, in whom I trust." Surely he will save you from the fowler's snare and from the deadly pestilence. He will cover you with his feathers, and under his wings you will find refuge; his faithfulness will be your shield and rampart."

PSALM 91:1-4

Sometimes, as a youngster, things would loom ominously bleak, and I would become terrified of exams and tests and toothache! Often I would be disappointed or hurt! And I remember climbing onto my Granddad's knee! He would put his long arms around me and hold me tight. Then I knew that nothing in the whole wide world could harm me. Oh my Granddad loved me more than tongue could tell, and everything would be alright!

"He will cover you with his feathers, and under his wings you will find refuge; his faithfulness will be your shield and rampart" (Psalm 91:4). Haven't you seen a mother-hen, gathering her chicks under her wings to keep them warm and safe from harm and danger? What a tender picture!

There is One who really cares about you and me! When we are troubled, hurt, disappointed, afraid, we must run into the arms of Jesus. Nothing in the world can harm us there!

DAY 23 - You Are Valuable

"Therefore I tell you, do not worry about your life, what you will eat or drink; or about your body, what you will wear. Is not life more important than food, and the body more important than clothes? Look at the birds of the air; they do not sow or reap or store away in barns, and yet your heavenly Father feeds them. Are you not much more valuable than they?"

MATTHEW 6:25-26

A rare visitor goes to Shetland from time to time. It's the yellow-browed warbler. Having been humanely caught, measured, weighed and ringed, it is released to continue the migratory journey from which it had been blown off-course. Later, if someone found the bird dead and returned the ring, valuable information could be gathered, concerning the bird's age, the distance flown, etc. Recently, an osprey, ringed at Loch Awe in 1998, was discovered in the Gambia, West Africa, in the stomach of a crocodile!

Some years ago, we woke up one day to find there had been a heavy, unpredicted snowfall. As my young son and I walked to school, we found scores of dead sparrows, lying under the snow-laden branches of the trees, at the side of our lane.

Jesus said, "Are not five sparrows sold for two pennies? Yet not one of them is forgotten by God. Indeed, the very hairs of your head are all numbered. Don't be afraid; you are worth more than many sparrows" (Luke 12:6-7).

God cares about every bird that He has made – not just the rare and magnificent ones, but the common ones too.

In these Bible verses, Jesus links God's concern for the birds to His care of you!

DAY 24 – Made Clean

"Cleanse me with hyssop, and I will be clean; wash me, and I will be whiter than snow."

PSALM 51:7

Is anything whiter than the snow? My mother used to boil her "whites" with a 'dolly-blue' in a big boiler. I still remember when she pegged them out, how brilliant-white they looked.

The Bible says:-

Job 37:6 God sends the snow.

Psalm147:16 He made it soft as wool (yet hard enough to sledge on!)

Job 39:22 There are treasures in the snow! God asks Job if he knew about them!

Did you know that each snowflake is different from another? And that each is perfectly symmetrical?

Psalm 148:8 Snow praises God and fulfils His word.

Daniel 7:9 Daniel had a beautiful vision of God on His throne, with garments which glistened like the snow.

David, the shepherd-king had committed adultery and even murder. When he realised the awful mess he was in, he repented with tears, and asked God to make him clean again – "wash me, and I will be whiter than snow" (v7).

We cannot wash away sin's stains. But Jesus can!

Is there anything whiter than the snow?

Yes – a heart that has been made clean by the Saviour!

DAY 25 – Jesus, You Please

"As the Scripture says, "Anyone who trusts in him will never be put to shame." For there is no difference between Jew and Gentile—the same Lord is Lord of all and richly blesses all who call on him, for, "Everyone who calls on the name of the Lord will be saved."

ROMANS 10:11-13

Kikreti (Big House) was a Brazilian Kayapo Indian from the village of Gorotire ('The People of a Long Time') on the banks of the Xingu river, by the mighty Amazon. He was a teenager, orphan, cheat, liar, wife-stealer, thief, and disliked by many of his tribe because he was as sly as the proverbial fox!

As the sun went down and made the tiny mud and palm-thatch roof-tops a lovely shade of pink, I would light my oil-lamp and sit on the dirt floor, with a number of naked Kayapo with painted, scarred bodies, lip-discs, necklaces of ancestors' bones, and gleaming, ebony-black hair as straight as a die!

Kikreti was usually present, sitting, listening to the few New Testament verses that were translated into his language. This is what he understood – "Long ago, the God of rain and thunder made the sky, moon, stars, forest, animals, rivers and everything! He also made people, but people disobeyed God, and did bad things. God became angry, because they needed to be punished! God had a Son – Yeyu (Jesus). One day, God sent Jesus to die on a cross of wood. He didn't deserve to die – He was good – but He took the punishment that everybody did deserve, because He loved them very much. And so we may be forgiven the bad things we have done, by trusting Jesus, the Saviour. One day He will take us to live in His beautiful Home to live with Him always."

One day, as he lay dying with tuberculosis, Kikreti said "Yeyu, gop ga!" "Jesus, you, please." And I know I shall meet him in Heaven.

Jesus, you please.

DAY 26 - Tell Me His Name Again!

"How, then, can they call on the one they have not believed in? And how can they believe in the one of whom they have not heard? And how can they hear without someone preaching to them? And how can they preach unless they are sent? As it is written, "How beautiful are the feet of those who bring good news!"

ROMANS 10:14-15

In a small town, in a Chinese province, a missionary told the simple story of Jesus. Many of her listeners sat on the ground, quietly absorbing this beautiful gospel story – His unique birth, His Holy Life, His healing ministry, His cruel death and wonderful resurrection! One of the listeners returned afterwards, to the missionary's home, a few miles away. Her mind was filled with this amazing story from the Bible, and she became troubled – troubled because she couldn't remember the name of the Saviour she had heard about for the first time. She just *had* to talk to the missionary! When she saw her, she tearfully begged, "Tell me His Name again!"

The Name of Jesus is very important.

Philippians 2:9 says it is, "the name that is above every name."

Acts 4:12 says, "Salvation is found in no one else, for there is no other name under heaven given to men by which we must be saved."

The Bible distinctly says that, "Everyone who calls on the name of the Lord will be saved" (Romans 10:13).

Have *you* called upon His lovely Name? He always hears and answers.

DAY 27 – Made Clean - Again

"If we claim to be without sin, we deceive ourselves and the truth is not in us. If we confess our sins, he is faithful and just and will forgive us our sins and purify us from all unrighteousness."

I John 1:8-9

We've had the privilege of owning two beautiful Springer-spaniels that have brought us such a lot of joy.

Many a visitor to Westward Ho! Beach would stop to watch Freckles digging – or, trying to dig – a deep hole, only to become increasingly frustrated, as the tide swept up his nose, while the sand disappeared under his paws! How that mini-tail would wag!

Jasper's doggy-idea of Heaven was to wade into a lake of mud, sit down in the middle of it, and look up at the sky. The worst thing was, though, he would choose the biggest cow-pat, roll in it and even eat it – as he would with a dead bird's carcase! Oh! The smell! So how to get him clean? Of course – throw a pebble into the sea, and after a dip or two in the ocean, out he would come – all the revolting smells gone – washed and sweet! It always reminded me of John 1:7, "and the blood of Jesus, his Son, purifies us from all sin."

However attractive we may be on the outside, you and I aren't clean on the inside, because of sin.

God loves us dearly, but hates our sin. Through the Cross of Christ, He has made it possible for us to be clean.

DAY 28 - Metamorphosis

"Therefore, if anyone is in Christ, he is a new creation; the old has gone, the new has come!"

2 Corinthians 5:17

Metamorphosis – a big word with a fantastic meaning. But the experience is earth-moving, mind-blowing, life-changing. It means a change of form by natural or supernatural means. Look at the world of nature – a pupa turns into an insect; a tadpole into a frog!

But the word also means a change by a supernatural act – and millions of people all over the globe have had that experience – they're called Christians! Becoming a Christian is a bit like waking up out of a dream. The old things have disappeared, and everything is new. It has nothing to do with turning over a new leaf. It has everything to do with beginning a new life. When the Lord Jesus Christ invades a person's life, He performs a creative act – a miracle of metamorphosis – an inside-out transformation. Just as the caterpillar's whole body dissolves in the cocoon and is re-constructed into a most exquisite butterfly, so our entire value-system, relationships, philosophy of life dissolves, and is reconstructed around Christ.

Metamorphosis is good for you! It reaches the parts that nothing else can! Such is life when you know Jesus – "if anyone is in Christ, he is a new creation; the old has gone; the new has come!"

DAY 29 – Satisfying Your Soul

"Jesus said to them, "I tell you the truth, it is not Moses who has given you the bread from heaven, but it is my Father who gives you the true bread from heaven. For the bread of God is he who comes down from heaven and gives life to the world." "Sir," they said, "from now on give us this bread." Then Jesus declared, "I am the bread of life. He who comes to me will never go hungry, and he who believes in me will never be thirsty."

JOHN 6:32-35

Tucked away in my mind, I have lovely memories of my granny's house – the warmth of it, the smell of it! There would, every day, be a bowl of rising bread on the hearth, by the coal-fire; and already baked, hot loaves just extracted from the old black-leaded oven. Perhaps that's why, sometimes, I choose to make my own bread. Nothing like it!

In Brazil, when my son went daily to the bakery for the warm bread, he was forgiven for not being able to resist the urge to eat a piece on the way home! In Uzbekistan,

Central Asia, bread is considered to be very precious. It's baked lovingly, shared generously, eaten slowly, and never wasted. It is the custom to take along some bread when visiting friends.

I remember one very stormy night on the Indian Ocean. The M.V. Doulos (a missionary ship) seemed like a cork on the ocean. Many of us were badly shaken from sea-sickness. Very early the next morning, there was a lovely surprise awaiting us! Lovely, warm bread rolls for breakfast! In the galley kitchen, the bakers had been up very, very early, working through the storm, knowing that many of us would need something plain and strengthening to eat.

To live without bread – what must it be like? Where there is famine, children, men and women long for a morsel of bread. Bread is nourishing. Bread is satisfying. That's why Jesus said of Himself, "I am the Bread of Life." His word is nourishing. The eternal life He gives is satisfying.

Jesus, bread of life, you feed me. You satisfy my soul!

DAY 30 – Like Mary

"In the sixth month, God sent the angel Gabriel to Nazareth, a town in Galilee, to a virgin pledged to be married to a man named Joseph, a descendant of David. The virgin's name was Mary. The angel went to her and said, "Greetings, you who are highly favoured! The Lord is with you."

LUKE 1:26-28

God was looking for a woman to play a strategic part in His great plan of redemption, and He found Mary! She was at most 16 years old, a teenage peasant from the grimy little town of Nazareth, which had a poor reputation in morals and religion. What made Mary God's choice of the mother of His Son – what were her qualifications? Humility, submission, piety, courage, modesty, purity, spiritual mindedness, her knowledge of scripture (Luke 1:30-38, 46-55; 2:51)?

This is the kind of woman that lodged Divinity. Fast-forward thirty four years, because we don't know a great deal about the intervening years. (We do read that Jesus grew in wisdom and stature and in favour with God and man - Luke 2:40.)

So, here she is standing as near to the Cross as she possibly could. On that dreadful, dreadful day at Golgotha, what unimaginable anguish must have almost overwhelmed her! She had to grieve silently, as mourning a crucified victim was not allowed by the Roman executioners. I can only dare to believe that she saw beyond that old, rugged cross, to Glory beyond, because of Simeon's and Anna's words of prophecy in the temple at the moment of His dedication (Luke 2). She had kept all these things in her heart and pondered them. Mary, the mother who had given birth to Jesus, who had served Him, loved Him, cooked for Him, washed His garments and cared for Him on a daily basis, when the carpenter's shop had been bolted, at the end of the day.

The Bible clearly states that Mary, in her song, refers to God as her Saviour. Even Mary needed a Saviour! When He hung on the Cross He died for Mary as He died for you and me.

DAY 31 – Immeasurable Love

"I pray that out of his glorious riches he may strengthen you with power through his Spirit in your inner being, so that Christ may dwell in your hearts through faith. And I pray that you, being rooted and established in love, may have power, together with all the saints, to grasp how wide and long and high and deep is the love of Christ, and to know this love that surpasses knowledge — that you may be filled to the measure of all the fullness of God."

Ephesians 3:16-19

Can I ever forget one particular moment, as I sat by the bedside of my lovely Dad? He was suffering greatly, and we were actually waiting for him to "slip away" into eternity. Suddenly he opened his eyes, took hold of my hand and said, quite clearly, "How do I love thee!" I was used to his unique dialect – his Derbyshire accent. (He had always spoken to us using "thee's" and "thou's"!) I think that was the last time that he spoke any sense. Within the next few hours he had left the world of the dead for the land of the living – and it seemed to me as though nothing, in the world, would ever be the same again! I remember a very trying time in Bible College, when six tiny rose-buds arrived by post, to cheer me up and bless me! My Dad knew and cared about me – and he loved me with an unconditional love. That's why, right now, I'm reaching for the tissues!

The Saviour's love is like that! But even greater! He knows all there is to know about us – and loves us, just the same! There is no love like the love of Jesus! He takes our hand and says, "I love you so very much!" He will never let us go!

What is your response to such love?

DAY 32 - Need A Bonfire?

"A number who had practiced sorcery brought their scrolls together and burned them publicly. When they calculated the value of the scrolls, the total came to fifty thousand drachmas. In this way the word of the Lord spread widely and grew in power."

ACTS 19:19-20

The air is filled with a peculiar warmth and odour. The fires crackle and spurt; there are big bangs and screams as the fireworks explode, thrusting all those multi-coloured sparks into the foggy November sky! It's bonfire night!

We read of a big bonfire in the book of Acts. Paul the apostle, had a very fruitful ministry in Ephesus – a wealthy, cultured and corrupt city. In fact, there was a spiritual awakening – a revival. There was repentance, and confession of sin; many people were healed, many were delivered from demon-possession, "magic books" were burnt – Jesus was magnified and His Word flourished.

The question is, do we need to have a bonfire?

What sort of trash are we hoarding in our homes? What about our magazines, books, videos, DVD's, CD's, newspapers and such? Once, when we were travelling, I bought a beautiful CD – lovely, peaceful music. When we got to the car, we noticed it was a New Age production, and quickly retraced our steps, to return it to the shop where it was purchased. "It was probably harmless," I can hear someone say!

Was it, though?

Before God can do a truly blessed work within us, the rubbish has to be dealt with.

Do you need to have a bonfire?

DAY 33 – He Desires Your Love

"Yet I hold this against you: You have forsaken your first love. Remember the height from which you have fallen! Repent and do the things you did at first. If you do not repent, I will come to you and remove your lampstand from its place."

REVELATION 2:4-5

Oh dear! The church at Ephesus had begun so well. It was a busy Bible based church which had seen revival blessing. But, after about 30 years, the apostle of love, John (now an old man in exile for his faith on the rocky island of Patmos) is given a stern message: a startling warning by the Spirit of God, for 7 churches – one of them, Ephesus!

'You have left your first love. Remember and repent! Otherwise, it will be as if you never were. I know all about your toil (effort that produces work at the cost of pain), labour, endurance, bodily wear and tear and your weariness. I have seen your patience, perseverance and persistence – but I have this against you – you have left your first love.'

What an indictment! They had become very right, very active, but loveless. Icily cold with a form of godliness and all the outward trappings. How sad. Probably attending lots of meetings; doing good things; right things; doctrinally correct but nothing in the heart. 'No love, the very first of my requirements,' says God.

Have you left your first love, the Lord Jesus? You may be knowledgeable of the Scriptures, well-educated, talented, skilful, successful, organised, practical – but, without His love pulsating through you; without an utter abandonment of everything, for a love that abandoned all for you – you are but an empty vessel; a resounding gong or a clanging cymbal. What a heartache to the Saviour!

He desires your love.

DAY 34 – Spiritual Healing

"I will heal their waywardness and love them freely, for my anger has turned away from them."

HOSEA 14:4

If I find myself losing spiritual vision, passion and enthusiasm, I am on a very slippery slope.

What may be the cause of our spiritual waywardness or deterioration? Possibly unwise associations, perhaps a friendship which may turn our hearts from the Lord Jesus. Maybe, worldly success.

Deuteronomy 8:10-19. These verses carry a warning to us to never forget God. What he has done for us, and all he has provided in His mercy. Just in case we say it was all down to us!

Perhaps there was no depth in our experience of God. The Word fell on rocky surfaces – we rejoiced, at first, but, in times of testing, we fell away. The seed had no depth (Luke 8:13).

It could be that we have become emotionally entangled with an unbeliever, wilfully disobeying God's command not to do so (2 Corinthians 6:14).

Do we give ourselves time to think about and to read the Bible? It is one of the daily duties and delights of the Christian. Mary sat at Jesus' feet and heard His word, and was commended by him. She chose "the better part" (Luke 10:39 & 42). His Word was given us that we may have hope and comfort; to instruct us concerning eternal life, and our journey from earth to heaven. It is food for our soul and the reading of it purifies our lives. Have we neglected this daily duty and delight? And what about prayerlessness?

Do we need to repent of any spiritual deterioration and turn again to the One who loves us so freely?

DAY 35 - A Heritage

"Sons are a heritage from the LORD,
children a reward from him.
Like arrows in the hands of a warrior
are sons born in one's youth.
Blessed is the man whose quiver is full of them.
They will not be put to shame when they
contend with their enemies in the gate."

PSALM 127:3-5

I am certainly and wonderfully blessed! God gave me one son! And what a son! I can't tell you how much I have learnt from him – so very much! From the moment he was born, in that tiny, tiny hospital in small corner of a Brazilian town, he heard the stories in the Bible, and was prayed over, day and night. In fact, I trust it's true to say that he has grown into the lovely man he is because he has always been wrapped up, so to speak, in a blanket of loving prayer.

As a Christian parent, I have a responsibility to praise God in the presence of my children (Psalm 145:4). In Joshua 4 the children of Israel were warned not to let their offspring forget God's dealings with them and never to forget His miracles. I also have the responsibility of reading the Bible with my children (Deuteronomy 6:7), passing on to them a love for His Word. The Bible is what they will need to know for the journey of life. Your children will live to bless you for introducing them to the Word of the living God, and the way of salvation.

I must also, with the Lord's help, practice what I preach! When I fail, confess; ask forgiveness; apologise when wrong; be totally honest; discipline in love, not anger; demonstrate faith in God's provision for every need, material or otherwise; take them into the fellowship of the church right from the cradle; and live out my life of faith with joy.

And we are to do our best to prepare them for 'winter,' that is, the struggles of life that will inevitably come, and to emphasise that our Heavenly Father is always with us.

In a foreign hospital awaiting stitches after an accident, "Don't leave me Mum. I'll be alright as long as I can see your face." And I learn another lesson: I shall be alright as long as I allow nothing to obscure God's face.

DAY 36 - The Service Test

"The third time he said to him, "Simon
son of John, do you love me?"
Peter was hurt because Jesus asked him
the third time, "Do you love me?"
He said, "Lord, you know all things; you know that I love you."
Jesus said, "Feed my sheep.'"

JOHN 21:17

I live but a literal stones-throw from the beach – can even see the sea from the bedroom window! Sometimes, at sunrise, the sun casts its beautiful rays upon the ocean, and all I see is a rim of shining gold on the horizon. If the tide is out, the white sandy shore dances and twinkles with an unearthly light.

Was it like that, I wonder, by Galilee's shore, on that unforgettable morning, when the risen Lord Jesus appeared, having prepared a barbecued breakfast of fish, with bread? You imagine the aroma! Some of the disciples had been fishing all night and were, no doubt, feeling disappointed and tired.

The stranger on the sands called out, 'Did you catch anything?'

'No.'

'Throw the net on the right side of the boat and you'll find a catch.'

They did so and amazingly brought in 153 large fish! John, at once, realised it was the Master – 'It's the Lord!' Peter couldn't wait to reach land! So, he threw himself into the sea, and swam ashore. Jesus called, 'Come and have some breakfast.' I am sure it was the loveliest breakfast they'd ever eaten or ever would eat!

I walked along that same stretch of beach, by Lake Galilee, and thought about the private conversation, after breakfast, just between Peter and his Master. The Master he had so recently denied having known, not once, but three times! Jesus then asked Peter not just once, but three times, if he truly loved Him! Jesus said, 'Feed my lambs, take care of my sheep.' In other words, 'Prove your devotion to me by serving me and following me closely.'

My love for the Lord Jesus is proved by my service.

Have I passed the service test?

DAY 37 - Pray For Them

"Brothers, pray for us."

I THESSALONIANS 5:25

All Christian workers who have been sent out with the gospel, to make disciples of all nations (including our own), are acutely aware of the need for prayer support. I look back to my missionary experience in Brazil. Knowing there are those who read between the lines of your prayer letter; who sense the home-sickness, weariness, helplessness, frustrations, weakness, loneliness, and utter dependence upon God, is a wonderful comfort.

That's how it was for me anyway, and now that the boot is on the other foot, so-to-speak, there are a few things I wonder about. Can I be relied upon to get to grips with information provided, through email, or the old fashioned prayer letter? Am I interested, that is *concerned*? Or, do I forget about it, lose it, leave it unread, unused? Have I a world map? Do I know where that missionary is living? What's the terrain like? Is it hot, cold, dry, wet? Do I earnestly pray that God will give facility in what may be a difficult language? How long does it take for that missionary to receive a birthday card? Incidentally, do I know the date? Do I encourage them with a letter, an email, a phone call, or even a small parcel with a treat? Do I know their present physical, material, emotional and spiritual needs? Have I thanked God for them today, as they perhaps wrestle with extreme temperatures or the lack of pleasant facilities? Have I asked God for their safety today, against the powers of darkness, and prayed that they will have constant fellowship with the Lord Jesus and experience His joy and peace in every difficulty; and that their lives will be as salt and light to the people to whom God has sent them?

DAY 38 – Be Wise

"But God said to him, 'You fool! This very night your life will be demanded from you. Then who will get what you have prepared for yourself?'"

LUKE 12:20

Jesus told the parable of the rich farmer. Why did he call him 'a fool'? (That is, evil, boaster, self-confident, empty, silly and stupid.)

Let's get one thing straight – he was not a fool because he was rich! He had barns, land and stock – and there's nothing wrong with that. He wasn't a fool because he was successful. He'd 'got on' and probably had a good social standing, because in Proverbs 19:4 we read, "Wealth brings many friends."

Neither was he a fool because he was a hard worker! He'd worked hard and long, ploughing, furrowing, sowing, planting and reaping. The Bible teaches us to do whatever our hands find to do and do it well. To be industrious, diligent and to rise early - these are all endorsed by God.

So, why was he 'a fool'?

First of all, because he left God out of the picture! He lived as though God didn't exist; as though God does not send the rain, the sun, or give life to the seed; forgot that all life is God-dependent. Secondly, he left others out of the picture. 'My' fruits, 'my' barns, 'my' goods! And he forgot that whatever we do affects others. Thirdly, he was a fool because he left death out of the picture. "I have plenty of good things laid up for many years." He lived as though there were no end – as if the death angel would never pay him a visit! James 4:14 says, "What is your life? You are a mist that appears for a little while and then vanishes." Fourthly, he was a fool because he left eternity out of the picture – forgot about the 'hereafter' – that, "man is destined to die once, and after that to face judgment" (Hebrews 9:27). This judgment will be just, individual and final. There is a hell to shun and a heaven to be gained.

Is it any wonder that God called this man a fool?

Make quite sure that when you meet God face to face He will not call you a fool.

DAY 39 - The Grace Of Simplicity

"Keep your lives free from the love of money and be content with what you have, because God has said, "Never will I leave you; never will I forsake you." So we say with confidence, "The Lord is my helper; I will not be afraid. What can man do to me?"

HEBREWS 13:5-6

My Mum's simplicity of life, contentment, cleanliness, hard-working ethos – no whinging, no moaning, really made an impact upon my young life. I never heard her say she 'wanted' anything, or even 'needed' anything. She honoured her elderly parents; trusted everybody; never spoke evil of anyone; never did a 'big shop'; always had something to give to all who entered the home – be it a chip-butty or a milky coffee! She never had a bank-account; never had surplus money. What money she did have was kept in a small red purse on top of the tiny American organ. Her whole life was one of sacrifice, and it left its mark on each of us that was blessed to call her 'Mam.' She lived for those she loved; and those she loved remember.

The Scripture above warns us to live a life free from the love of money, and to be content with what we have. We see in all the world around us that the love of money is a root of every kind of evil (I Timothy 6:10). We may never have a big bank account for that reason! (God knows what's good for us – and we could be drawn into temptation!) He says to us, "Never will I leave you; never will I forsake you."

He is all we need!

Let's be content with all we have - "godliness with contentment is great gain" (ITimothy 6:6).

DAY 40 - Essence of Eternity

"Then Mary took about a pint of pure nard,
an expensive perfume; she poured it on Jesus'
feet and wiped his feet with her hair.
And the house was filled with the fragrance of the perfume."

JOHN 12:3

The Bible Dictionary tells us that, "The rose-red, fragrant ointment made from the dried roots and woolly stems of the spikenard plant was a favourite perfume of the ancients. A precious ointment (Mark 14:3), it was and still is transported in an alabaster box to preserve its fragrance. Because it had to be imported from Northern India, it was extremely yet understandably costly."

Mary's sacrifice was a *loving* sacrifice (love recognises love), because she loved her Master.

Mary's sacrifice was a *lavish* sacrifice, because she poured out ALL the ointment, and had to use her long hair to wipe off the surplus.

Mary's sacrifice was a *lasting* sacrifice. We read that the odour permeated every room in the house. It penetrated the walls and curtains. Probably, the fragrant aroma clung to the robes of all present – and, probably, long after the event, it lingered.

I ask myself, "How long is it since I showed my love to the Saviour, by some lavish, sacrificial act?"

Like Mary's perfume, the odour of Christ's Sacrifice has remained as sweet as ever, throughout the centuries, and those who come into contact with the Rose of Sharon (Song of Solomon 2:1) will carry with them the fragrance of eternity.

"Moment by moment give your grace

That I may fragrant be,

To permeate the courts of time

With essence of eternity."

It Was For You

It was for you that paradise I left,
The glory of my Father's throne,
That you might dwell forever there.
Your flesh I took,
My all forsook,
It was for you, my child.

It was for you my back was turned on glory
When on the holy mount,
Arrayed in Hermon whiteness
Alone I stood –
My heart assured
Of death for you, my child.

It was for you the garden with its loneliness,
The bitter dregs I drank
That you might taste the wine.
The beads of supplication,
The mocking crowd's derision
Were all for you, my child.

It was for you, the cross with all its burden;
The shameful death I died
That you might live eternally.
The sinful condemnation,
My Father's separation
Were all for you, my child.

It was for you, the empty tomb's abiding glory;
The Easter morning dawned
That you may be forever justified.
My resurrection life,
My Spirit's breath
Are gifts for you, my child.

It was for you, ascension into the land of endless day,
The return to God my Father's home,
From whence I came.
'Tis there I wait,
At Heaven's gate,
I wait for you, my child.

It is for you that when, once more, the Father bids me go
In glorified and risen power,
With Heaven's host of angels,
I'll share with thee
Heaven's majesty,
It is for you, my child.

- Mavis Sutton

On mission in Northern Ireland in 1960. Mavis is on the right.

Living in the Amazon Jungle with Kayapo Indians.

Mavis, Alfred and Tim preparing to return to Brazil in 1980.

Ministering in Asia, as part of an OM women's team, 1997.

By an Amazon tributary, where previous missionaries had been killed some years before.

ACKNOWLEDGEMENTS

Sincere thanks to Pat, who began the work of typing up the manuscript. And also to Tim, who finished that work and helped with editing.